ROSETTA CENTER MINISTRIES

Strong Woman, I Dare You To Submit

Marriage and Relationships God's Way: A guide for couples and singles

Dr. Michele W. Reapsmith

The book is committed to the restoration of marriage and living a full and rewarding life with your spouse. It is a guide for couples trying to strengthen their union or singles anticipating marriage. God Bless You!

Dedications

First giving honor to my Lord and Savior Jesus Christ for loving me so much that he laid down his life for me. I will always in my thoughts, speech and behavior uplift His name in all things that I do. I believe that I CAN do all things in Jesus Christ... (Philippians 4:13).

I must freely give reverence to my husband, Jimmie Lee Smith, Sr and my son Jimmie Lee Smith, Jr., both of whom, I love with all my heart. God bless them both.

To my beloved Mother, Etta D. Williams (1946-2006), whom I miss dearly and pray that we will meet again in Heaven one day. Oh, what a joyous day that will be for me. Thank you Momma for giving me life and allowing me to share some of your life with you; and I treasure our moments together more now than ever. Losing you has taught me more about contentment and treasuring the time we have more than anything else. Also to my Father, William H. Reap, Sr., I love you. I would like to give a special dedication to my Mother-in-law, Rosa Kay Smith for just being a sweetheart.

Further, I want to give thanks to all of the Pastors in my life whom have provided guidance in shaping my Christian experience. My childhood through adulthood under the care of the late Reverend John D. Mason Sr. and the current Reverend Lawrence Curtis from the First Emmanuel Baptist Church and Pastor James Lindsay from Mt Nebo, all in High Point NC.

Last but certainly not least, I thank all of the Rosetta Center Ministries' members and followers. They have made this book possible because of their unyielding encouragement and support. All of you have inspired me more than I can tell you and I appreciate it deep in my heart. Amen!

Table of Contents

	Page
Dedications	2
Preface and Dialogue	5
What is the Problem?	7
Good Wife According to the World or Word?	15
First things first	15
Why are we all looking for Husbands	18
Making the Right Choice	23
Married women	25
Your Reflection	33
How should we treat each other?	36
So What Do I Get for All This Work?	38
Submission	41
Why Can't I Be Equal?	46
Relationships and Love	49
Day to day living	52
Marriage Quest	56
Decide for the Right Reasons	56
Finding a "Good" Man	61
Restoring Your Marriage	69
Commitment	72
Communications	74
Forgiveness	76
Growing Spiritually	77
Resolving Conflicts	79
Romance and Sex	79

Husbands and Wives Do so Much Wrong	*80*
Challenges	**82**
Extended Family	*82*
Outside Children	*83*
Money Matters	*84*
Unreasonable Expectations	*86*
People Viruses	*87*
Reminders	**90**
Pray	*90*
Never quit	*91*
Tame your mouth	*91*
Start a union	*93*
Strength and Endurance	*93*
Children	*95*
The Do(s) of a Good Marriage	**97**
Husband – Do these things without fail	**98**
Wife - Do these things without fail	**100**
Dr Chele's Final Commentary	**102**

Preface and Dialogue

I am the founder and Pastor of Rosetta Center Ministries which was inspired first by a message sent to me from God and second in loving memory of my Mother (Etta D. Williams, 1946-2006). The ministry began in 2009 and was called Rose Memorial; also named after my Mother. The purpose of the ministry began as a means to spread the word of God in a manner that was not intimidating and easy to understand. I have been told by several people, both young and old, that they have read the Bible but do not understand it and further, did not know how to apply it to their everyday lives. I thought this had to be frustrating for someone who wanted to know Jesus and felt helpless in doing so. One of the first things I learned about Jesus is that one of his goals was to teach the Word of God to everyone. This was the goal of Rose Memorial as well.

Of course, being in this world, I faced many obstacles. The first being I am a woman and at the time, a woman that did not understand the value that God had placed in me from the very beginning of time. The second obstacle was the view of the world regarding Christianity and women in the ministry. I had to learn what God had for me to do and disregard the many tricks that had been placed by the enemy before me. After studying and learning how I should approach my ministry along with so many trials; I had to turn to God alone for direction and He provided as usual.

After some time, I change the name of the ministry to Rosetta Center Ministries and devised a New Mission. We are still all about the business of God and our main goal is to spread the Word to all that will hear it. But there was something that was missing. I had received a message in my sleep telling me that I needed to pay more attention to the family; especially the wife and husband roles. It was very clear after that time what I needed to do. Accordingly, Rosetta Center Ministries is one that offers relationship restoration and building through the Word of God. I have found that many of our relationships are failing because of our attitudes, mindsets, and a simple failure to apply guidance from God.

Through our counseling sessions, messages, websites, blogs, spoken words, and individualized attention to all our members, readers, and subscribers I have been able to reach many people particularly women. What women are beginning to realize is that they are responsible and obligated to God for the ultimate well-being of their households. The world and its definitions would have you believe that you are weaker compared to men although God made no comparisons. My ministry helps men and women understand that there is no comparison between men and women. We were made differently by God and shall remain so. God has laid out what each of us as a sex is responsible for in our lives. Anything else that is added is wrong. That, my fellow Christians, is the bottom line. We must take the Bible and re-learn what we believe we have already learned.

There are so many things that we have to deal with as Christians living among so many that are minions of the devil. But we must find peace knowing that God, through His sacrifice of His Son and Jesus' sacrifice of His life; we already have the victory. Now we have to claim it! I have experienced firsthand what a poor or non-existent relationship with God can do to a family. My parents were divorced and I personally suffered a failed marriage at age seventeen. My calling is to educate couples in relationship restoration through the Word of God and assist them in understanding that no problem is insurmountable when you are walking with Jesus.

My sincerest prayer is for all marriages to succeed and for all relationships to be founded in the Word of God and obedience. I know through grace, mercy has already been bestowed on us; we simply need to recognize it and be faithful. God wants us to succeed and He has provided all the resources we could ever need for an abundant life according to his Word. Amen!

Let's start learning how to restore our relationships through Jesus!

What is the Problem?

Many of us claim to be Christians; we claim to know what the Word of God is and we claim that we are walking as Jesus walked. But, how can we make all of these claims and not have Faith in what God is telling us by being obedient? I have found that many of our problems are the result of simple disobedience. If God said it then it is so, correct? We all believe that, but in our lives we are not able to successfully operate within God's Word. Do you think that this difficulty was an accident? God knew that we were going to face obstacles therefore he gave us guidelines in some cases and commandments in other cases to ensure that we could make it in our lives. Noncompliance has consequences. If we will realize that there are consequences for disobedience and we continue to be disobedient; then we should expect consequences. That makes logical sense to me.

The problem as it was revealed to me is a two-fold problem compounded with all of the in-depth knowledge that the world has taught us during our lives and our desire to create marriage relationships outside of God's Word. If we just sit and think about those two issues, we will automatically began to realize how the two things could never work together. God created marriage and the corresponding rules that go along with it; therefore it cannot work unless we follow the rules.

I am going to define what being a wife means in accordance with the scriptures which includes what I call God's "job description" for us. This job description is mainly directed at and focuses centrally on women. We have done a fantastic job of allowing people in this world to direct us in our relationships by insisting that we follow a different plan than what God has laid out for us. We have mimicked what we have seen on television; we have idealized what we have seen in other relationships; we have made up our own fantasy relationships; we have determined how we should act in accordance with the world; and to be honest what we have *actually* done is made it impossible to have a successful married relationship. I have given this message many times to groups of men and women and have met with agreement and opposition. But in my belief, it should be difficult for anyone to oppose what God has directed unless this world is guiding that opposition.

Accordingly, we must be careful to avoid people and ideas that oppose God.

It is ironic that many of the Christians that come to me for counseling are men. They normally begin their conversation apologizing because they know I focus many topics on women. But of course, I help them to understand that not only do women have a job description, but men do as well. Surprisingly to many women; men are very eager to understand their role as a husband and they want to walk closer with Jesus. Women will get very defensive at the number of tasks that are in their job description but it is no comparison to the job description of our husbands. As we progress, I will further explain how difficult a husband's job really is as commanded by God.

Normally the men are concerned that they are doing something to provoke their wives' negative behavior and they feel bad because they want their wives happy. More times than not, the husbands have not done anything to provoke them; but the wives have a mindset that is not allowing them to achieve happiness and contentment in their relationship. Seeking additional blessings before offering thanksgiving for the ones we already have is definitely not pleasing to God. Often times this is the source of discontentment and negativity from the wives, therefore making the husband's role more difficult because he tends to feel inadequate.

This is where I began my *mirror check*. You have an obligation to check yourself at all times. If you fail to do it appropriately and consistently; then you are going to fail your family and yourself. It does not matter whether you are a man or a woman; you have to check yourself. There is only one way to do that. You might have guessed it, through the Word of God. Every single day you take a look in the mirror to make sure your clothes are squared away and your hair is perfect, right? And if that mirror shows you anything that is out of place, you immediately fix it! Before you leave the house to go to work, school, church, or just about anywhere you take a quick look in the mirror. Accordingly, that tells me you trust your reflection in the mirror. A preacher I follow once said, "…have you ever popped your eyes out and turned them around to look at your body?" The answer is *no*, because it is not possible, therefore we have come to trust the reflection in the mirror.

We cannot have a successful relationship until we check our spiritual selves in the mirror. This is a different kind of mirror and it is simply your Bible. You can use your Bible to see a reflection of your spirit. And if there is something that is out of place, you can fix it. Remember this, you are comprised of a three part being; the flesh, the spirit, and the soul. God has taken care of the soul and it is up to you to take care of the flesh and spirit. Your flesh should never be leading your spirit, but your spirit should always be in control of your flesh. When you begin to change your mindset and allow your spirit to lead according to God's Word; you will see how things will change for you. Simply the way you present your attitude and the way you think about things we'll be very different.

I received a question from a nice young lady who was a wife and Mother who asked why it is so easy for your spouse to list out of your faults and cannot see their own faults. That's an easy one… a *mirror check* has not been done. Are the wives receiving benevolence from their husbands and returning that same benevolence? Do the husbands love their wives like Jesus loved the Church? Remember that charity means love, which was defined by God and again by Jesus. Love means to give; whereby love is sacrificial by its very nature. *(Numbers 30:13 and 1 Corinthians 7:3).*

We are quick to let our spouse know their faults because we are being led by the enemy (world) not God. We have a wonderful and glorious opportunity to go to the Lord confessing and coming away clean with a chance to do it right. As a wife or husband, it is not your job to find fault, but to restore. Your wife or husband is your brother or sister in Christ as well as the folks at your Church. I am not sure why married folks forget that bit of fine print. Therefore we have to restore them with meekness and not arrogance. If you have an arrogant spirit you will fall prey to the same temptations that you are presenting to your spouse. You are never to confront your spouse or any other Christian with an arrogant spirit. *"A bruised reed shall he not break… (Isaiah 42:3)*, therefore never kick anyone when they are already down.

Lastly, if you have an unbelieving spouse, you must hold up that spouse and not leave them *(1 Corinthians 7:14)* AND move away from evil speech and be kind to one another *(Ephesians 4:31-32)*. The reason why your spouse is not listening to you is the manner in your approach. Do it the right way and get the appropriate results. If you are blessed enough to be the saved half of your marriage, do not be one of those arrogant Christians that believes you are better than someone who is not saved. Part of your duty as a believer is to let your light shine and encourage others to accept Jesus as well. This is especially true for your spouse.

Subsequently, what we have to do as wives, husbands, and married couples is take back from this world what God gave to us in his Prophecy. God bestowed upon married couples a bonded union of divine love that cannot be broken except by death. The world has no right to it, it belongs to us, and we are going to have it.

What do we do now? I am going to begin defining the job description of the wife then we're going to learn how to treat each other because these are the most important things in a successful relationship.

I will also define what we should be looking for in a *"good"* man, if anything. I recognize that some women believe that their husband is supposed to do an infinite list of things for them as the world has described it to them, but I am going to show you all of the wonderful things that you already receive that has nothing to do with this worldly belief. Many women also believe that the husband is more responsible for the relationship than the wife; I am going to show you that this is a myth as well.

Remember this, if you do not remember anything else, you have got to change your attitude and the way you think about your relationship in order to change the relationship. There is no other way to begin your restoration. We are going to repent and get on another path to righteousness in our lives and our marriages.

Good Wife According to the World or Word?

First things first

Over the course of time women have forgotten to read and read again, the "job description" as God has set forth. Remember when your earthly job gave you form to sign stating that you have read and understand the employee handbook and your job description? This little form of acknowledgement simply let your employer know that you understood and was going to comply with the rules and regulations of the company. Additionally, they let you know what would be the consequences for noncompliance. You were perfectly fine with that and decided to comply to keep your job.

You take your employment job description very seriously and make it a point in letting everyone at work know what is and is not included in your particular set of tasks. You make sure people are clear when they ask you to perform a task, "that is not in my job description." Do you ever simply do the task that is not in your job description? And if you do assist someone else; do they "owe you one?"

Think about that job description. You have learned it and can recite what is contained in it. Ask yourself, have you done the Word of God the same way? Have you approached God to learn your job description in life? Do you know it? Can you recite it? But most importantly, if someone asks you to do something that is *NOT* in it; will you let them know with quickness, "that is not in my job description?"

Why has it been difficult in your life to learn and accept your Holy job description as a Christian and as a wife or husband? You have to recognize, study, and consistently seek *"what is right."* What we know is right is located in the Holy Bible *only*. Inter-mingling what you think or what your friends tell you will always be inappropriate unless it is founded in the Word of God in its entirety. All of the scriptures of life and the light must be activated in our everyday existence to work in the name of Jesus. It is further ironic, how we always find a way to *"pick and choose"* what we want to apply to us and we leave out what we do not want to hear or deal with in our lives.

The *"pick and choose"* approach is a recipe for failure. How do you know what is right if you have no idea what is wrong? The Word of

God is a complete guide. Complete means ALL. One example of "*pick and choose,*" which has destroyed a lot of relationships at home, work, and Church, is the scripture that tells us that our husband is our *head*. Why has this brought about so much controversy? Well, you know that I am going to tell you. Mainly, this is misconstrued by men and women who have not gathered God's Word in its entirety. This has been a scripture that men have beaten up women with for hundreds of years. And women use it as a defense mechanism to show their rebellion against control. But if you look closer, which we will, "control" has nothing to do with the "head". This is yet another one of those "*pick and choose*" Bible readers. Ladies, do not become angry and further remove yourself from God, simply pray for men and ask God to reveal truth to them. Gentlemen do not use any part of God's Word to demonstrate dominance over your wife, pray for your spiritual growth and understanding of God's reverence for your wife. *WE WILL COME BACK TO THIS ONE FOR SURE!*

Why are we all looking for Husbands

Should we be out looking for husbands? If you are consistently looking for a husband, please stop. Get your looking glass out, look yourself in the eyes and say, *"I am not going to turn over one more stone looking for a man but I am going to wait on the Lord."* If you have asked God for a husband and He sees fit to send you one; you can stake the farm that He will send one to you with no effort on your part. The hard work does not start until after you get that husband you keep asking for every time you pray. The mistake that we make is we can never just wait on God to move on our prayers. I know it is what we want and we want it right now, but be patient! Ask yourself what happens if you want it now and God has decided that it will be several years before you receive this particular blessing in your life? What should you do? You *should* do nothing and continue to wait, but many do not! What women will do is find somebody that fits their "Mr. Right" list and marry him as soon as possible. Afterwards she is wondering why there is so much hell created in her life.

It is not going to work simply because you exercised some earthly law or your human desire. Really? Yes, really! Marriage is put together by God and only He can sanctify it. You can cast your vote on amendment #1, #7, #10, or #100; but it cannot change or improve what God created. And who better to send you the right husband and direct you in the ways of marriage then the One who created it?

In addition to my work at Rosetta Center Ministries, I also teach college level accounting and in speaking with one of the more seasoned professors; I mentioned marriage and some of the relationship work that I am doing in my ministry. He told me very boldly that no one should ever get married because over half of all marriages end in divorce. My response to him was "if God put it together then it cannot be taken apart by divorce or any other means." Of course I met with some opposition but the truth is the light. You can marry 25 different men and if every single one is the wrong one; it will not work. These men are wrong because God did not send them to you. When God gives you a husband; everything about that marriage is going to be right. It may not seem right to the world and sometimes it may not seem right to you, but no one and nothing will be able to come between that union including people, divorce, or anything else. Let them try!

I implore you to stop actively seeking a husband because it is not going to do you any good. Stop wasting your time. Believe that God is going to give you everything that you need including your husband. Have you ever stopped to think that you are not ready to have a husband yet? This may be the reason that you do not have one. God knows when that time is; just be patient. Getting married before you are ready is double trouble. I am a living testimony and I will never move ahead of God again; it just does not work!

I had some ladies speak to me about waiting for God to bring them a husband and in the meantime they have become very bitter and upset because it is taking too long in their opinion. Now they have a bad attitude and say they do not want a man at all. I see this more in career women, highly educated women, and just plain mad women. Somehow they have come to believe that they do not need a man, which is untrue. This is not rocket science, God has already given us guidance on how to decide if we want to have a man or not, therefore this is not new. Stop saying such things because you do not mean it. It would be better to say, I am upset that I do not have a husband. This is a more honest statement.

The explanations women give me about not being able to find a man are more ironic than the fact that they are looking for a man or have given up looking for a man. The main reason is they cannot find a man that is on their level. What level would this be, exactly? Next they tell me finding a man who is not intimidated by their job, education and income is impossible. My response is HOGWASH! When you are blessed with your husband; the husband that God sends you, he will not care how much money you make; he will not care how much education or money you have; and he will revere and support you in all that you do because he will love you as your husband. A husband by definition in the Bible cannot be a success in his obligation to God where you are concerned if he does not treat you the same way Jesus treated the Church.

I'm going to share with you my experience on this subject with my husband. I am an extremely strong woman with a will of iron and I try with all that I do to exemplify that in my marriage and household. Sometimes I am borderline "hardheaded," which my husband does let me know with quickness. I decided years ago that I was going to be a career student due to my love for school plus I wanted to see just how far I could make it. I was going to be a collegiate professor, career woman and in recent years a minister; all while raising a family. My husband, other than wanting me to rest, has been the greatest support system that I have had in my life. He believes that I can do anything that I set my mind to do and he continuously encourages me. When I am successful he praises me and when I fail he comforts me. Over the years his behavior and care towards me has been motivation to praise and thank God everyday for blessing me this way. With that out in the open; later I am going to show you the beauty of strength and submission the way God said it! And yes, I, my degrees and my career submit to that man every chance I get. Hallelujah!

I tell many people about my husband and the things that he does, but he is not perfect and neither am I, but we have God working in our lives and that makes a difference. The things that I do not like about his behavior are minimal when compared to the love that we share. All husbands have the potential to be as God commanded and we have to wait for their acceptance of Jesus. Women have told me that all husbands do not behave that way, but I am here to tell you that *all* husbands do behave that way. Are we speaking of husbands of the world or husbands of God? If you have chosen a husband that was of your own works; be very careful and go to God in all humbleness asking him to forgive you. This was not what you were supposed to do, hence the hell in your house. God will restore you and make it right, but you have to repent first. You cannot take something that belongs to God and do with it what you may. Marriage is certainly one of those things. This works the same for you when you become saved after marriage and finally see the reasons for so many bad years; now you can make it right. When you confess and ask God to take your life into his grace; he takes it all including your marriage.

Making the Right Choice

As women and wives, our goal is to walk as close to Jesus as we can whereby sealing our family's destiny under our watch. Later, I am going to reveal a list of what we must do in our relationships as women and a way to accomplish those things. Remember, the decision of wife should not be entered into lightly. If a woman decides that she will not become a wife, then she has a different set of rules. *1 Corinthian 7:32-35* reads as follows:

***32** But I would have you without carefulness. He that is unmarried careth for the things that belong to the Lord, how he may please the Lord: **33** But he that is married careth for the things that are of the world, how he may please his wife. **34** There is difference also between a wife and a virgin. The unmarried woman careth for the things of the Lord, that she may be holy both in body and in spirit: but she that is married careth for the things of the world, how she may please her husband. **35** And this I speak for your own profit; not that I may cast a snare upon you, but for that which is comely, and that ye may attend upon the Lord without distraction.*

This basically means, women who decide to be single are tasked to give their attention to the Lord instead of a man. During your bachelorette period get as close to Jesus as you can and serve him faithfully and without distraction. Prepare yourself to become a wife in the future. For right now, be content in the Lord and remove yourself from the temptations of the world as you are commanded. Once you learn how to serve the Lord; you will *KNOW* how to be a wife!

An old Bishop once said, *"…the single person should be abiding in joy, not out wrestling with singleness. Enjoy it. Rather than spend all your effort trying to change your marital state, you need to learn to develop in the position where He has placed you."* I agree with him. Again, I say wait on the Lord!

Married women

Women that choose marriage have a list of tasks, attitudes, speech and behaviors to accomplish while becoming a "good" wife. First let's discuss how we were created and why. *Genesis 2:21-24* gives us the creation story of woman including that we are made from man, therefore we are woman. What men and women forget is that we are one flesh, not all of these separate persons that we have created in our imaginations. Stop that! Women were created for the purpose of being a help mate to man. Later, you will learn how to do that with certainty and grace. God gave woman to man as a Glorious gift. How wonderful it is to be a gift to our husbands especially from God. Of course, with that kind of honor we do not want to do anything to tarnish that Glory.

Or maybe we do? It can be difficult to tell by the way some women behave. That is something that you will have to do the *mirror check* to find out.

Just think about how you treat other gifts you receive. What about a gift from your husband? What about a gift from your children? What about a gift from your family? These are all gifts that we take care of and put away for safekeeping. We are angry if anybody touches those gifts. Therefore, when we think about gifts and how precious they are to the receiver; we need to view ourselves as something as precious as the ultimate gift. Be proud because of your stature as a gift by letting your light shine through your relationship and family. I will show you how you are a direct reflection of your family through your exuberance of pride regarding your blessed status.

I know this is a lot of responsibility, but God made us in such a way that we are willing to do all that we need to do to deserve the honor. Remember if you are *willing* to do something, you do not complain or show weariness at the task. We make it a point sometimes to let everyone know how much work we have to do in order to keep things together. This is not fair! Are you trying to lay some guilt trip on your folks? If so, stop it! You are only doing your job. My Mother used to say, *"be seen and not heard!"* This means you are characterized better by your works than by lip service. If your relationship and family are together and blessed; everyone will know how hard you have worked without a word from you. Let your light shine!

Maybe by now you are thinking that you might want to be single, right? Although, you do have the option to remain single as we see in *1 Corinthians 7:35*; don't you think that the world's definition of marriage is driving you to feel that way? What we do not realize is when we walk with the Lord, we want to do the things He has asked us to do. A woman in *1 Corinthians 1:40* will be happier if she remains a virgin and single then if she is disobedient. Remember before you became sexually active, how you did not have as much to worry about in the flesh? These decisions bring on trouble in our lives if we do not approach them correctly and in the name of the Lord. God gave us these commandments for our own protection against our weaknesses.

I remember when I was in the military and all of the rules that we had to follow. These rules were designed to protect us and allow us to do our jobs in the best and most efficient manner. The only time that we found ourselves in any trouble or discontentment was when we were noncompliant with the rules. All other times we were happy and content because we had nothing to worry about. All of the drama that was brought into our military lives was brought on by us. Our attitude regarding the rules was the major determining factor of how we lived. The laws of marriage operate the same way and for similar reasons. God has given us laws for our protection, safety, and the best possible married life to live. He has laid out very clearly what we are to do and how we are to do it. The great thing about God is that he gives us a choice. I caution you to make that choice wisely! Your very life and the quality of that life depend on your willingness to be obedient.

We have discussed the idea of getting married or deciding not to get married. If we do decide to get married there are things that are going to be obvious on the outside and inside. One important thing is how we look on the outside, which gets overlooked for some reason.

The Bible is very clear in *Proverbs 31:22* regarding the type of adornments or clothing that the wife wears. She wears the finest tapestries in the Bible, but of course now, we would wear the best clothing that we could find; it would fit perfectly and make us look beautiful and sexy for our husbands. Only for the husband and no other man *(that is one of the rules)*. So when the world tells you that you can look any way after you become married; they are highly mistaken. Sometimes my use of the word "world" means the enemy or devil, but in this case, I am going to say when your "friends", especially your girlfriends, tell you that it is ok, there is a motive for it. You must know for yourself what you need to do for success in your relationship from God's perspective. You must also know why your girlfriend has plenty of negativity to share with you regarding your relationship. Your friends should always offer love and kindness in their advice to you in the name of the Lord. If you find that the words that are offered by your friends are destroying you; then they are of the devil, plain and simple. This is the job description of the devil; to steal, kill, and destroy. There is no life in this behavior and you must beware! Give your husband as much "eye candy" as he desires and rebuke the naysayers.

Here is something that many women have asked for advice about because they have allowed their friends to manipulate their mindset and attitude regarding their husband and marriage in general. One of the first things I ask is if they have sought guidance from the Word of God? Many times the answer is *"no."* As a result of not seeking God first, we fall prey to the work of the enemy. An example of this behavior was a Christian wife that had a friend which could not wait to tell that she had seen the husband in a place where he may not have needed to be. The Christian wife was distraught and attacked her husband as soon as he got home. The husband explained that he had been at a meeting with his boss that afternoon, but the wife was not hearing it. After some time she came to me and told the whole story. I could not wait for the wife to finish because there were a few questions I needed to ask her before moving on. One, did you seek God? Two, how did your friend approach you with the information? Three, what exactly did you say to her in response? Four, how did she respond to your response? Five, did you tell her what you were going to tell your husband? Six, why did you not believe your husband?

Let me tell you why I asked her all of these questions. I needed to know where her Faith was at the time. If she did not have Faith enough to go to God first; then we had even more work to do which had nothing to do with the information she received. I needed to know how her friend approached her because that would tell me if she was approaching her out of judgment and contempt. It was important for me to know what her response was to the friend because this would tell me what kind of relationship they had together; good or evil. The friend's response to her response was important because when a non-Christian woman is referred to a scripture, prayer or anything that is not of this world they will become instantly angry. Next I wanted to know did this friend get her to say what she was going to do when her husband came home. I wanted to know in order to understand what her motives really were. Lastly, I needed to know why she did not believe her husband. Our Faith in our husbands through the Faith we have in God protects us from the enemy or nosy friends. That same great Faith endures us through our relationships. Faith is not an option.

After speaking with the Christian wife she left understanding the motives of her friend and how it is imperative for her to never allow anyone to bring negativity into her relationship. This holds true even if the information they bring to you is correct. Fortunately for the Christian wife, the information she received was false. But that would not have mattered because her first priority is her husband and marriage. We could stay on this subject for many chapters but the bottom line is we have to understand and accept our place as a Christian wife. We do not allow the world to have an open invitation to disrupt something as beautiful as what we have created in the name of Jesus.

Your Reflection

You have learned the requirements that God has listed for us including: how to feel; how to behave; how to care for children and husbands, and even how to dress. What you may not be aware of is if we accomplish the requirements successfully they will be reflected in our family. In *Proverbs 31:23-31* we see that our works that we have performed for our husbands are seen and widely recognized when they leave our presence. Have you ever looked at a strange man and knew right away that he was married? You know this because of how he carries himself; how he is dressed; how he behaves; and the mode of his conversation. A man that now belongs to a good wife carries himself poised and upright because of that total confidence and trust he has in his wife with his heart (*Proverbs 31:11*). He moves like he is on a mission. And moreover, people can see the level of trust and confidence that you, the wife, has lived up to in his life. Remember how important that "safety" of trust is to your marriage. How he is dressed is an indication of your work as people will see that his suit is clean, his socks match, his tie is on straight, and he has all the necessary gear in his pockets (keys, Chap Stick, phone, notes etc…). The husband is prepared for his day. A man's behavior is a powerful reflection of you. He is not going to *look* like he's available; he *looks* like he is married.

Ever wonder why so many women are attracted to *your* husband? It is because you have done all that you are supposed to do and it is a beautiful thing! Lastly, you are seen in his conversations because he cannot speak without commenting on how wonderful you are and/or something that you have done or said. These things will be repeated in his conversations. The world will know who he is because of who you are to him, his wife. Just thinking about it makes me want to shout in the aisles. It is truly a beautiful thing!

Accordingly, your children will have the same reflection of you. When they leave your presence they will behave differently than other children who do not have a Faithful and caring Mother doing her works in the name of the Lord. This is not to say that children of non-Christians are misbehaved, but there is something about a Christian Mother's children. They will carry themselves differently, they will dress differently, they will speak differently, and they have an advantage of knowing appropriate behavior; not saying they will always act appropriately. Of course, Christian children are said to be worse than other children by the world. Have you ever thought about why people say that? First, the children of obviously saved parents are expected to behave in a certain way or "better," but people forget the fact that they are still children. Secondly, the devil has a way of getting to us through our children. Unsaved people will try every trick in the book to lure our children out into the world. This puts a lot of pressure on our children that we have to be prepared for while rearing them. Although, the devil is at work, this is still a direct reflection of how we have raised them in the Lord and the corresponding desire of the world to take them away. Be proud that you have riled the devil up and be prepared to continue to fight him for your family.

The characteristics of strength and honor are called clothing for the wife and we must put these things on each and every day of our lives (*Proverbs 31:25*). When we speak there must be wisdom that pours from our mouth and kindness must always be our purpose. Do you find yourself practicing these traits? If not, why not? You must realize God made us out of love; gave us to man out of love; he made the ultimate sacrifice out of love; therefore everything we do should be out of love. These things can be seen in your family when you are not around. As you are doing all of these things; you will be praised first by your children who will bless you and secondly your husband will praise you as well and lastly your fear and obedience to God will manifest into praise outside of your household *(Proverbs 31:28-31)*. Through your work and obedience; you will have it "going on!"

How should we treat each other?

Sometimes it is difficult to really get a handle on how we should treat each other. This is referring to our husbands, our children, our loved ones, our friends, our brothers and sisters in Christ, and anyone else for that matter. We are going to discuss how we should treat our husbands as matter of concern. The first thing that we need to do is reverence our husbands in all that we do. This has become a point of debate and controversy in our society of modern day women. I am not certain how this came about other than the fact that the devil is very busy. Reverence is simply that we respect our husbands from God's perspective. Why would you not want to do that? Show respect for your husband in all the things that you do. We are never to make him ashamed or else God perceives us as "rottenness in his bones (*Proverbs 12:4*). Do you think about cancer when you imagine rotten bones? Who wants to be viewed that way? It is not difficult to make sure that we carry ourselves appropriately as wives; it is a mindset and attitude. Would you disrespect God? God has asked you *not* to be disrespectful to your husband either. If you say that you respect God and you do not respect your husband; you are being disobedient and God is not pleased.

Of course this subject of respect brings about some problems. Today's women will say that men do not respect them therefore they do not deserve respect. Unfortunately for us that is not what the Bible tells us regarding the subject. It is not about what you think and how you believe you should behave; it is all about what God has commanded us to do. A deeper question is what are you providing for the disrespectful man to respect? How do you carry yourself? Are you portraying yourself as a virtuous woman; one to be sanctified and revered? What is in your conversation? Are you following Christ's teachings? Remember your *mirror check*. What is on the inside of you and more importantly, what does your spirit look like? After you have been honest with yourself, re-ask what are you giving the disrespectful man to respect? Man does not naturally disrespect women because it is not of God. There must be something else in the mix. *Mirror check!*

A major obstacle that I run into more often than not is people who will not be honest with themselves first. If you are unable to adequately see yourself, there is no way possible for you to be a vital member of a successful relationship. You have got to work on you before bringing anyone else into your messy situation. The backbone of a relationship is honesty and it starts with you. Do not come up with all sorts of rules for your life in order to justify bad behavior; just come clean and work on you as a person. Start with your spirit and your flesh will follow. *Mirror check!*

So What Do I Get for All This Work?

Women must first understand what the man's role is in our marriages and lives. Women have made all kinds of rules for men that they simply are not going to be able to live up to as men. Not to mention, who are you to define the very existence of man? God did that already and your job is to accept it. God has been very specific regarding the unconditional love and care a man must give to his wife and children. And yes, our husband's are the head of us as wives (*1 Corinthians 11:3*). Let's stop with the "*control*" issue. Both men and women need to get a handle on this issue. The Bible tells us that God is the head of Christ; Christ is the head of man; and man is the head of woman. Every person except God has a head. This includes everything you do and everywhere you go, work, school, church, recreation, concerts and everywhere else. There must be order otherwise there will be chaos. And we can see there can still be chaos if the head is disobedient. This just makes sense and I am frustrated that we have taken God's Word out of context again to fit our own purposes. It works well "as is." Once again we see the *"pick and choose"* approach does not work.

Wives do not grasp the level of responsibility and obligation to God that man has upon him with this head position. The scripture states that man is our head just as Christ was the head of the Church or the body. Remember the body? The body that was formed when God made woman is not just the woman; it is both the man and the woman together. Our bones are their bones; our flesh is their flesh; and we are one (*Genesis 2:21-24*). How would an intelligent person view their body without a head; and consequently view their head without a body? It just does not make any sense at all and cannot be sustained. This Holy organizational chart is a good thing. One cannot function without the other and each has its own tasks. The head and the body, if they are working together as God planned, are a magnificent structure.

We know that man is to his wife as Christ was to the Church. Jesus loved the Church (the body) and he was the Savior of the body for which he laid down his life. Jesus practiced self-denial and made the body an intense object of his concern. All He lived for and thought about was protecting and preserving the body. So as a husband has the same responsibility and obligation to the wife. He must love his wife as he loves himself as he loves Christ. He ensures that his wife is happy. A husband desires with all his heart to save his wife from wanting, affliction, and pain. He naturally protects her and anticipates her needs. These needs are of great concern to him and providing for them is his priority. A man is under strict obligation and command from God to provide his wife comfort during trials and tribulations just as Christ did for the Church.

A husband loves, cherishes, and nourishes his wife "even *as the Lord the Church*" (*Ephesians 5:25, 29, and 31*). A husband will give himself for his wife and sanctify her in all things that she is presented gloriously Holy, clean, and perfect (*Ephesians 5:25-27*). You cannot just do anything to a man's wife because he will protect her with his very life. A wife must realize and understand that these obligations are not easily accomplished and a man must work hard to be successful. This is the reason why God insists that we give him reverence in all that we do.

Submission

Subjecting and submitting ourselves to our husbands is a hard pill to swallow for some women. The main reason is due to our total misunderstanding of the meaning of submission. For example, what if you went to the DMV and found all of the signs had been changed to Spanish? How would you know what to do? More than likely you would follow someone else who was ahead of you. The more logical thing to do is acknowledge that you do not understand and ask for assistance learning the subject. Confusion and disobedience is what has happened to women who fail to gain a coherent understanding of submission. Again I am finding that it is a sore topic because of the *"control"* issue. And yet again, submission has nothing to do with control, even less than the "head" thing. The way you are thinking about submission is a worldly viewpoint as defined by the world and you have to let it go and ask for assistance in your comprehension.

The Bible tells wives to submit to their husbands and also to submit to one another (*Ephesians 5:21 and Colossians 3:18*). The word "submission" simply means either yielding yourself to another or getting consideration or approval from another. That seems mild in the grand scheme of things. Wives you are to submit to your husband only. This means you are not to have sexual relations or intimacy with any man except your husband receiving agreement from him only. How can this be a bad thing? How can we have so much of the devil in us that we make something so beautiful a point of argument? The other part of submission is both for marriages and Christians alike, we are to ask for consideration and obtain approval or agreement. The wife, husband and Christians should *not* strike out on their own without fellowship (sharing) and make decisions only following approval or agreement. Yes, we have taken it all out of context and we need to bring it back down and be obedient. Why would we want to do anything without consulting with our husbands first? Everything we do affects our marriage in one way or the other. It is much easier to move forward if both the wife and husband are moving in the same direction.

Let's talk about how beautiful submission is between a husband and wife. We are to "doll" ourselves up, present and give ourselves to our husband. You are not only blessing him, but he is blessing you as well (*1 Peter 3:5*). But do we think about it that way? Women have the nerve to refuse to submit their bodies to their husband and subsequently use themselves as some sort of punishment for their husbands (*1 Corinthians 7:4-5*). Wrong, wrong, wrong! You have now DIRECTLY defied God and opened the door for predatory behavior from your husband. Is making your point that important that you will risk everything?

You do not have control over your body and he does not have control over his body. We share power over each other's body and should never deprive each other. The only way to keep your body from your spouse is through *mutual* consent in times of prayer and fasting (*1 Corinthians 7:5*). God knew what a bad thing this was and gave us a ruling on it. So even if you are in a period of prayer and fasting; if you BOTH do not consent; submission still takes place. By the way, this is also how God says to keep your spouse from wandering. God really does have an answer for everything!

Please stop making your own rules for marriage. *Romans 10:3* reminds us directly that we practice ignorance when we create our own righteousness and not "*submit*" to God's righteousness. Let's not practice ignorance. There are just some things that we *MUST* do in order to obtain the benefits of the Glory of God. Anything else is an attitude of rebellion. Do you really believe that God would tell us to do something that would make us unhappy or is not beneficial to us in some way? No, not at all. There was only *ONE* punishment that God administered to all and that was in *Genesis 3:16*. Everything else is on you. You get to choose how you will progress in life and what your Glory will look like. Choose who you will serve in your life and in your house (*Joshua 24:15*). I know you have heard it before, but I dare you to try God this time. Something better will happen in your days to come, I promise.

Now that we realize that our husbands do not "*control*" us, not even in the Bible, but there has to be order in our lives; do you feel any better with this added knowledge? Our husband was given authority by God over us just as Christ was given authority over the Church. Authority means that you have to take total personal concern of everything that is in your care. Your husband is supposed to be concerned about you wholly including your body and mind. Let him do his job offering him support and not resistance. I am so thankful that I have my husband to exercise his authority over me by caring for me.

Why Can't I Be Equal?

Why would you want to be equal to a man? Maybe it is something that someone told you that makes you believe that men are better somehow. Well maybe I can change your mind. You are a wife and you want to be equal to your husband, right? The immediate question is equal how? Do you want to both have children and maybe breast feed after the children arrive? Do you want to have his natural muscle strength? Maybe you want to have a square face like your husband? What do you want exactly? This may seem trivial but the concept of equality is just as trivial if you think about it long enough. God created woman as a beautiful and functional part of His plan. In *Genesis 2:20-25,* God created us to help man but how can we do that if we are exactly alike? Plus, you obviously have no clue of how precious you are to God. Jesus once told a man who had just called Him "good" that there is nothing good but God (*Mark 10:17-21*). Then we find out that God believes that wives are also "good" in his sight. Can you imagine that the only thing that is good in the universe viewing you as good (*Proverbs 18:22*)? Right now every woman reading this book should be jumping around singing hallelujah! You should feel good and honored.

And yes, it gets much better and more beautiful. We are the crown of our husbands whereby making him a king (*Proverbs 12:4*) AND the best part is that God compares us to rubies (*Proverbs 3:15*). There is absolutely nothing that a man can desire that is more precious than you or could ever compare to you. Our value was explained using rubies in the Bible because there was nothing else that people would understand that had immeasurable value. There was only one other thing that was compared to rubies and that was wisdom. A wife and wisdom, the most valuable things a man can have in his life. This is what you want to give away so easily? I am going to carry my value just as God laid it out for me as more valuable than anything my husband could even imagine. Try and top that!

I realize that many of you still want to be equal to men. You want to have equal pay for equal work and you want to be treated as a man is treated in the world. Ok, that is fine for the world. You may demand things of the world that may or may not draw you away from God and these things might make your flesh happy. But I am telling you that you will be much happier living as God sees you and not only will your flesh be happy, but you will be happy in your spirit. A wife and her husband are *one* flesh with two spirits. The wife has her role and the husband has his; they are not identical in the Bible and rightfully so. We are able to do the same jobs and learn the same information here on earth and in some cases excel at those functions, but our roles in the eyes of the Lord are vastly different. We are not able and should not aspire to change God's plan.

The bottom line regarding these control and equality issues is we must respect our husbands as the head of the body as we respect Christ as the head of the Church. As far as control is concerned, Christ did not control the Church; he cared for the Church; he protected the Church; he worried about the Church; he provided for the needs of the Church;

he led the Church in the right path; and he died for the Church. This is the definition of head. Submit to your head and do not try to be his equal. Think about it this way, if you were all of a sudden equal to man, according to God's value of you, this would be a downgrade. We need to focus on an upgrade!

Relationships and Love

Sometimes we fool ourselves into believing that we are doing everything that we are supposed to do but our husbands will still not act right. I am going back to the question I asked earlier; are you acting right? Do the *mirror check* before you began to slice into your husband. It is entirely more likely that both of you have some work to do. Be quick to restore your husband and refuse to do anything to destroy him. You have committed yourself to love, honor, and cherish that man; therefore you must lift him up even when you do not believe he deserves it.

Why do we get married if we are not willing to make the commitment? Ruth gave a great definition of commitment in *chapter 1 verse 16-17*… *"For where you go I will go, and where you lodge I will lodge. Your people shall be my people, and your God my God. Where you die I will die, and there will I be buried. May the Lord do so to me and more also if anything but death parts me from you."* That is powerful and such a commitment is one that we must strive for in our marriages. We are one Holy flesh when we become married and should be willing to commit wholly. Remember we are to love our husbands with Christ-like love. This love is undying and is with all of our heart, soul and mind (*Matthew 22:37*). Do you love your husband in this manner? Have you told him the depth of your love for him? If you cannot positively answer this question, then your primary quest should be to gain a different answer.

Another strong point about real love can be found in *1 Corinthians 13:1-13* showing us that you may have the ability to speak in tongues; be a prophet; gain God's level of understanding; have all the Faith; and can move mountains but without love you *ARE* nothing. You have to know love and practice that love everyday of your life. How many days this week have you encouraged your husband as he leaves the house for the day? Our love has to be "patient and kind" barring enviousness and boastfulness to our spouses; neither being arrogant or rude. How many mornings have gone by that you have not spoken a kind word to your husband or how many nights have you gone to bed angry? God has provided us with the power to remedy this behavior, but it is useless to have it available to us if we are not using it.

Are you keeping your commitment to the Lord by entrusting Him with your life and believing He will do what He says He will do? Your heart has to be fully devoted and unswerving to Jesus in order to be obedient and receive his Glory (*1 Kings 8:61*). When the Lord lays it down for us like that; I am certain that we do not have an option but to be obedient if we want what is ours. We keep asking for husbands, but our hearts and minds are unclear. Remember the ladies I spoke about earlier that were simply getting tired of waiting for God to send them a husband? Their lack of commitment made them grow weary. We have to maintain our strength to maintain our commitment.

We have to believe in our hearts that we cannot grow tired from waiting on God, especially when we are doing the work as the Lord has commanded. And know that we are going to be rewarded just as He promised in Heaven and on earth (*Galatians 6:9*). Women were directed specifically to keep ourselves strong physically so that we may continue to press on caring for our family in the name of the Lord (*Proverbs 31:17*). We were told that if we just persevere that our plans would succeed and we would reap a good harvest. Therefore we know we must plant good seeds to get good fruit. When are you going to get tired of bad harvests?

A woman once told me after hearing my *commitment* message that she did not feel that her husband was as committed to her as she was to him. She felt her commitment was a waste of time. I asked her if she loved her husband because she would not have been speaking with me if she did not. She agreed that she loved him and I sent her to read *2 Timothy 2:3 and 1 Corinthians 13:6-7*. Sure there are going to be times that are going to be hard; you may not understand why you have to go through some things; but you continue loving AND continue working for God AND you will have peace in knowing that you are protected. Your husband's commitment probably is just as strong as your commitment, but as women we mistakenly want our husbands to feel exactly like us. Again, we are not exactly alike. Do not try and force a square peg into a round hole! It does not fit.

Day to day living

Your day to day living has to begin with confidence in the things that Jesus has told us. We must have confidence in ourselves; confidence in our abilities; confidence that Jesus is going to do what he says he is going to do today; confidence that the peace that God has given us will endure all day; and confidence that everything will be alright internally and externally. The Lord said have *I not commanded thee? Be strong and of good courage… (Joshua 1:9)*. This is exactly what we need to do at all times; believing that God is with us. Our relationships have to be confronted with the exact same confidence. Our Lord and Savior Jesus Christ is with us in the midst of our relationships and we only have to trust and believe him. Our confidence in our marriage is a testament to our Faith.

Some people say that you can't be too confident in your relationship because that will make you arrogant. I am not speaking of arrogance, but I am talking about the courage that is given to you by God to sustain your relationship. For example, if someone is intruding in your relationship you have an obligation to remedy that situation.

Let them know without a doubt that your relationship is not going to tolerate such an intrusion. Call God in on the situation and leave it there because it is over. You have to believe it otherwise it does not work. And Oh yes, Dr. Chele says, *"my marriage is the best to me and for me. I am going to keep it in front of God and you cannot intrude. Try and stop me! I am boldly letting the world know right now, you cannot have my husband or my child. I bind you and all your minions with the ultimate power and authority that God has given to me. Be gone from my Holy union!"* Make a statement and hold to it. Have confidence in your Faith.

Let's say that you have been the best wife that you can be; you have done all the things that the Bible has instructed you to do, but you are finding that your husband is not doing all the things that the Bible instructs him to do. If you have not experienced this; you will. How do you handle the situation? First, you have a conversation with God letting him know what is going on; how you feel about it; and ask Him to provide guidance in your spirit. Remember the spirit guides the flesh. So do not allow your flesh to strike your husband in the head when he does not behave the way you believe he should. Alternatively, you should have a conversation with him telling him the same things you told God.

Many women say that their husbands do not listen to them, but that does not mean that you stop talking. Your husband hears you but maybe not in the way that satisfies you. Keep talking! We know by now that since husbands love us like Christ loved the Church; he aches when we ache; he feels what we feel; he hurts when we hurt; he is joyous when we are joyous; and he is sad when we are sad; therefore we must continue to partner and share with our husbands always. It is imperative for the relationship. Further, know that your conversation must happen with the understanding that you are a woman and you feel like a woman; and he is a man and he feels like a man. They are not the same. Do not expect your husband to react to situations the same way as you do. It is an unrealistic expectation and will only cause trouble in your relationship.

Marriage Quest

We are going to discuss how to survive your quest for marriage and finding a "*good*" man. The information presented earlier in the book has to be accepted and you have to come to terms with the fact that you are just going to have to do some things. We understand the order of things and now we need to ensure that we have a solid grasp on it and we are willing to operate fully within the Word of God by being obedient.

Decide for the Right Reasons

Decide if you want to be married. Make sure that you are not in love with the idea of being married. Getting married for the wrong reason is a drastic life-changing mistake. This is a decision that could not only destroy your life, but the lives of your spouse and future children. Do you want to be held accountable for such a decision? We are taught by society that getting married is a fantasy and we dream about the fairytale wedding, when in fact the marriage has nothing to do with the wedding size, colors, number of attendants, location, or cost.

So many businesses have made millions of dollars on the concept of the wedding. Who is paying attention to the marriage? It is not hard to get a grasp on the marriage if we seek the Word of God. But how many times is that really done? We should not be planning the fairytale wedding, but the lifetime marriage.

Let's talk about these reasons. Getting married is and should be a life altering event in your life. Our marriage should consist of a close relationship with God giving us staying power; maturing love; shared values; and an unwavering commitment. Marriage cannot be entered into as a means to solve another problem. For instance, if your current home life is not so good; getting married could be a way out. I realize that family life can be difficult, but do you really want to base your marriage on the fact that you were trying to run away from your parents or something else? Remember we have to fix ourselves before we bring anybody else into our situation. *Mirror check!*

Next we have the group of people that get married because that's what they are supposed to do, or so they believe. Maybe they have been in a courtship for many years or maybe they were paired up by their parents. Since all of the loved ones agree, they proceed to get married and afterwards they have multiple serious problems. These problems are present because they did not base the marriage on the choosing of God and they did not really understand who they were as people at the time. You should always take the opportunity that God gives you as a single person to serve Him and learn yourself prior to getting married. For those of you that have been married before or are still married; have you ever thought about what would have happened if you would have waited?

Believe it or not there are some women and men who believe that they have the power to change another person; therefore they get married in order to make that change. But it is a fool who believes that they can change anyone except for themselves. Any change made in an individual must be made by the individual. A marriage based on this concept is doomed from the beginning. The man and woman will not be working towards the same goal or the right goals. The one flesh will be continuously eating at itself leading to destruction.

What about that group of saved people that are single and *nipping at the bits* to get married so that they can have sex? You know that you are not supposed to have sex outside of marriage, but do not get married for that sole reason. Sex is a benefit of marriage and is a beautiful exchange of love between two people. It is not fair to either the man or the woman to take that out of context. What is truly unfair is one of the spouses may actually love the other only to find out that it was a marriage of convenience. The burning question is how long do you believe this type of marriage is going to work? The only thing that is happening in this situation is they are fooling themselves. They're not fooling God because He knows their heart. So what is the point? I guess the point is people feel less guilty about having sex if they go ahead and get married?

One of the worst reasons to get married is to avoid being lonely. There is a huge difference between being alone and being lonely. Loneliness can be eliminated through seeking Jesus. He will be your comforter when you feel lonely and further, He will be all that you need until God sends you a husband. Finding someone to simply fill a hole in your life is not going to be fulfilling to either of you. Remember when you are alone (single), you are told to serve the Lord without distraction. The devil will confuse you by making you believe that you are lonely when in fact, you are just alone. I have found that both men and women fall prey to this little trick. Sometimes the feeling of loneliness can be physically sickening, but do not let yourself be tricked. You do have a comforter and you must utilize Him as such. Loneliness is another one of those things you have to work out within yourself prior to getting married. Just a quick side note: you can also be among people or married and feel lonely. *Mirror check!* Fix that before you get married.

Finding a "Good" Man

I am going to tell you again to wait on the Lord and be glad while you wait (*Psalm 27:14*). Many of you are not so keen on waiting, but I know that Jesus is a fortress that can protect you and not allow you to become weary. Just hold steady and your husband will come without you doing a thing. The Bible tells us that grace is "bestowed" upon us meaning we do not have to do thing for it. Jesus just works that way and you have to have Faith to believe it. Faith allows you to wait. The word "wait" means to rest with expectation. We expect God to fulfill everything He promised; therefore waiting for Him should not be difficult in the right mindset.

Have you ever wondered why when we get ahead of God things do not come out quite right? If we allow God to move ahead of us and lead; a clear path can be seen because He has already made the way. Trouble will manifest in our lives when we leave God behind. Always keep Him in front and you will never have to look back for Him. It is impossible for him to leave us or forsake us, unlike when we leave Him so many times (*Hebrews 13:5*). Be glad that God has His own ways and

His own timing (*Isaiah 55:8-9*). What a mess we would be in if his thoughts were not higher than ours? Give over control of the husband hunt to God.

The Bible did not say that you should be looking for a husband; it says "a man that findeth… (*Proverbs 18:22*)." We should *NOT* be looking high and low for a man, but asking God to send us one when we are ready and in His good time. But do not worry about it after you ask for it…God will not withhold any good thing from you… (*James 1:17*). All good gifts are from Heaven including your husband.

You just asked God for a *good* man, but what is a *good* man? Do you know? Do you have a "Mr. Right" list? Did you ask God? We know that everything God created was good and a saved man is "real" *good*. He is not saved by his works but by his Faith, therefore when a man accepts Jesus Christ as his Lord and Savior there is a magnificent change in him which allows him to become the husband that God has obligated him to be for you. This is a beautiful thing! A saved man will fear God and out of that fear will be obedient. This fear that he has for God is an obvious reverence for God and his Word. A real love and divine spirit in him will be obvious in everything that he does. He will be offended by anyone or anything that is in opposition to God. This obedience will ensure that he will treat you the way God has commanded. I cannot imagine anything as beautiful as this! Next, I am going to tell you exactly what a *good* man is and I am going to suggest that you hold on to your seat.

A *good* man maintains his spirit by studying God's Word (*2 Timothy 2:15*). He desires the approval of God and is not ashamed. He requires of himself the knowledge of God's Word firsthand and does not simply take other people's word for it. This man will do God's will and knows that God give us shepherds (Pastors) but Jesus is Lord and he trust Him. *This man's immersion in the Word will ensure you a Godly husband.*

A *good* man will not only keep God's Word in his mouth, he loves the Word (*Psalm 119:165*). He will take the Word and apply it to your lives when trouble comes, and it will come. Your *good* man will know the Word because he realizes that his family does not live by bread alone (*Matthew 4:4*). He will keep God first in your life so that you can make it successfully through trials and tribulations. He will guard your joy with the Word of God. Whatever is within his heart will surly come out of his mouth. It is a blessing that a *good* man has God in his heart because love can only come out of his mouth. God is love in its purest most real sense. *This man's love of God will ensure you that he knows how to be a Godly husband.*

A *good* man supplies his family. A man that does not work cannot eat, so a man has to sustain himself and his family (*2 Thessalonians 3:10*). We noticed that Paul in the Bible found work to sustain himself even though he was an apostle and preacher. He did not let others take care of him. Many men will allow his flock to sustain him, but a *good* man will not. The Bible calls a man an "infidel" if he does not provide for his family (his own) and he denies his Faith. *This man that will work for his own as God commanded will be a Godly husband.*

A *good* man will pray with and for his family and all others in their time of trouble and offer thanksgiving and praise in times of peace (*Psalm 77:2*). He will have a consistent and open line of communication with the Lord. He confesses his sins and knows how to repent. He will pray for you and himself requesting constant direction from God. He desires to be guided on the right path in all that he does. *This man that knows the words to pray directly to the Kingdom of God will be a Godly husband.*

A *good* man brings others into the fold. He allows his light to shine bright so that others may see it and desire the Savior. This man is not ashamed to shout his beliefs for all to know. He is anticipating the crown that he will receive for turning many people to righteousness (*1 Corinthians 3:13-14*). Bringing as many people as he can to the throne of grace is an important part of his service. *This man that is concerned about building up the Kingdom will be a Godly husband.*

A *good* man knows that God did not mean for him to be single or incomplete. God made everything in pairs and commanded them to be fruitful. A *good* man will obey God when he finds his wife and nothing will ever be placed above her (*Genesis 2:18 and 2:24*). You will never have to worry about playing second fiddle to anyone that he has forsaken including his parents, siblings, friends, etc… He wants to be obedient and pleasing in God's sight. He will never enjoy another woman's self as he knows that only a husband and wife are able to enjoy the benefits of submission. He will not desire another woman. *This man that is Faithful to God and you will ensure you a Godly husband.*

A *good* man will lead his family in the ways of the Lord (Genesis 18:19). He will not allow anyone to take his place as husband and Father in the admonition and nurture of the Lord (*Ephesians 6:4*). He respects and honors his obligations fully. Additionally he realizes through study of the Word that he is held accountable to God himself. *This man that is a God-fearing leader will ensure you a Godly husband.*

A *good* man is in constant service to the Lord and insists that everyone in his house participates in that service (*Joshua 24:15*). He will look for ways to deliberate that service. This man will be Faithful as an example to his family to ensure that they are Faithful as well. And he is wise in his thoughts and behaviors by seeking out wisdom (*Ecclesiastes 7:25*). He does not allow his family to follow false prophets not knowing the difference between good and evil. Through his service to the Lord he avoids sin at all costs casting away any evil partakers (Proverbs 1:10). *This man that seeks wisdom in the ways of good will ensure you a Godly husband.*

A *good* man is not jealous, arrogant, or foolish. He is humble in his ways and does not care if he gets credit for his works because he knows where his treasure is laid. This man will be more concerned with the content of his heart than his outward appearance, fortune, or fame because he knows that God knows his heart (*1 Samuel 16:7*). It is within his heart that you will reap the benefits of your good works. *This man that is humble and works to please God will ensure you a Godly husband.*

Now you have the definition of a *good* man; the next major question that I have for you AND must get an honest answer: Are you *READY* to be married to a "*good*" man? I would like every woman reading this book to dust off your "Mr. Right" list and ask yourself if any of the *good* man attributes listed above are on *YOUR* list. I am certain that you noticed the type of job he holds; how much money he makes, what kind of house he owns; his education level; or anything of the kind is NOT on the "*good*" man list. Do you believe that you may have been asking the Lord for the wrong kind of man? This can be alleviated simply by consulting the Bible for your requests. The Bible is clear regarding the *good* man. "*The steps of a good man are ordered by the*

Lord' and he is happy about it. He may fall but the Lord holds him up with His hand (*Psalm 27:23-24*). Maybe it is time for you to ask the Lord for a *good* man and not "Mr. Right!"

Think about all of the things we were discussing in our job description especially reverence and submission. It should be easy to submit to a *good* man, right? Our lack of understanding and rebellion are the reasons we have such issues following God's lead; whereby making it difficult to follow our *good* men, although we are constantly begging for one. A woman that is following God does not have a problem following her man that is also following God. By the sheer dynamics, both of you are going in the same direction. How much more easily do you want it to come to you?

Restoring Your Marriage

Marriage is not an institution created on earth; God created marriage as the unit that would increase the human race as God saw fit. The value that God placed on marriage required certain commandments or laws to keep it Holy and sanctified. A man and a woman are incomplete alone and only represent part of the Prophecy. God was displeased with man being alone and created woman (*Genesis 2:18*). Once woman was created she became one flesh with the man by God. This is a union that no one but God can disjoin. Although, we see millions of couples in divorce court all over the world every year; it is still in direct conflict with the Word of God. How can this be pleasing to God? Has anybody asked for restoration? Have you or your husband fallen and decided to give up instead of asking for restoration? If so, you are displeasing God and making a solid attempt to interfere with the Divine Plan.

Remember your parents leave you their houses and riches, but a wife comes from the Lord only (*Proverbs 19:14*). And that wife is a good thing for the man and he gets God's favor. Marriage is a connection like no other connection because it is blessed by God. The only way to break the connection is by death. Remember Ruth's commitment?

We know that the Lord also spoke of divorce and he said very clearly that what God had joined together no man could put apart. And unless there is some sexual immortality a divorce cannot take place (*Matthew 19:3-9*). I recall a married couple telling me that they used to love each dearly but now have fallen out of love. HOGWASH again! Love never fades (*1 Corinthians 13:8*). This fading love was never God's love. Oh my, what if God decided that he did not love us anymore, it just faded? What a predicament we would find ourselves in today! And divorce goes against the very nature of man and woman because they cannot function appropriately without each other. They are incomplete without each other (*1 Corinthians 11:11-12*). I know some of you are saying that you are doing just fine without a husband, which may be true to some degree. But the fact still remains that you are incomplete.

Some women have told me that they have not asked for restoration because they are unable to get over the fact that their husband was unfaithful. I will say that you must forgive him, first for your sake and second for the sake of your marriage. We must forgive in order to be forgiven. Remember to do your *mirror check*! I know that many couples are faced with adultery problems and they must take it to God; repenting and asking for forgiveness and restoration. The Lord instilled sexual desires in every man and woman, but we are meant to enjoy ourselves together as husband and wife only. Being a man and a woman sexually is a beautiful gift from the Lord and we must be thankful for it by keeping it sacred between the husband and the wife. God instructed us to do this. The marriage is honorable and the marriage bed is "undefiled" meaning no one but a husband and his wife will share it for as long as they live (*Hebrews 13:4*). *Hebrews* goes on to state that we must learn to be content with what we already have, therefore do not need go outside of our marriage looking for anything extra. You have everything you need bestowed upon you now. I will go one step further and say that if God did not give it to you then you do not need it. Hallelujah!

Commitment

How strong is your commitment to your marriage? When you decided to get married you not only made a vow to your spouse, but you made a vow to God to keep his solemn law about marriage. Remember the *"put asunder"* thing (*Matthew 19:6*)? This verse basically defined commitment beyond the depths of our understanding. Not even the ones that made the vow can break the commitment. Only death can break the bond you made when you got married. Renew your commitment each and every day in your prayers and with your spouse. Ask God to renew your marriage everyday and love each other the way that you should.

Yes, you can get a divorce and the world can tell you that you are no longer married, but guess what, you are still married. Keep that in mind the next time you want to dissolve your commitment to your wife or husband AND God. You gave your word to be a husband and a wife before God; keep your word in all the things that you do.

You must work hard to restore your commitment to each other because this commitment is an essential part of your relationship. Hard times will come and you will feel like your commitment is being tested, hold strong and go to God. These are the times that you will wonder how strong your commitment is to your marriage. But always keep in the front of your mind and in your heart that this commitment is more important than any commitment that you have made in your life and it must be honored. Also understand that your commitment to your wife or husband is what keeps you together and must be preserved.

Your commitment and Faith is not something that operates of the world; it is something that is deep in your heart and cannot be removed by any trick of the enemy. You must ask God to restore your mental ability to understand the oneness that you have with your spouse. Ask God for forgiveness because He knows that we will be tempted; He knows that we will fall; but He also knows our heart and will restore us to the level of commitment that He is pleased with according to his Word. Remember your marriage promises to your spouse including: I will love you; I will cherish you; and I will honor you for all the days of my life? How would you feel if someone made those promises to you and then took them back? *Mirror check*!

Communications

You must communicate with your spouse all things large and small. Keep all crazy "corrupt" language out of your mouth. Only speak life and encouragement to your spouse with honesty (*Ephesians 4:29*). Your words should bless your spouse. Does this mean that you have to be serious all the time? Not at all. I have found that Christian couples that are living the Word of God have a blast together and are always laughing. My husband still keeps me in stitches, which is one of the things I love so much about him. Even when I feel down, he makes sure he finds a way to make me smile. This is that "*good*" man thing we talked about earlier. It does work when you let it. So go ahead and talk to each other; play with each other; and tell a joke every now and then.

Remember when I said that men and women are different? Here is where you will test yourself during the communication process. I know talking is difficult but you have to make yourself do it. Sometimes when I am trying to be the "serious wife" or the "serious Mother" *and* my husband is still clowning around *and* frazzling my nerves; I keep talking. I promise it gets through to him, maybe not in the way that I would prefer, but the goal is to consistently communicate and agree. Remember we are going to approach things differently and that is perfectly ok. The fire that you are able to start with little words is enormous (*James 3:2-12*). Use what you have! **KEEP TALKING!**

What about if you are angry about something; then you are to talk more? Wait! You are *talking* not *arguing*, there is a difference. You love your spouse and there is a quality way to speak to him that is not offensive or ugly. And never agree to disagree. If you have to leave the conversation and move into prayer returning later to the conversation, do that. The two of you *must* agree on everything even if it is a compromise. Remember you are one flesh whereby prevention of split movements in opposite directions is imperative for survival. You have to be on one accord always.

The most important thing about married people communicating is learning that you are one and you should always say "we." This little word means so much to reconcile your understanding of the "union" of marriage. And remember to consult each other in submission when any decision affects either of you, because everything affects both of you.

Forgiveness

Learn to forgive your spouse. If you ever want to have a successful and strong relationship, you must learn how to forgive and seek forgiveness as well. You begin your path of forgiveness by renewing yourself with Christ and your spouse. This is the only way that you can relieve serious problems in your married and spiritual life. Remember the spirit leads the flesh and not the other way around. Keep in mind that when you are acting in a sinful way to your spouse, meaning prideful attitude, arrogance, rudeness, selfishness and other things, that you must ask for forgiveness. There's no other way to gain restoration. You have to be willing to allow Jesus Christ to intervene. You have to believe if you commit your marriage to God and trust Him that He will restore your relationship (*Psalm 37:5*).

We are not allowed to judge or condemn else we will be judged and condemned, but if we forgive then we will also be forgiven (*Luke 6:37*). God commanded us to forgive (*Matthew 18:35*). Please do not think that you can dish out forgiveness when you feel like it or when you believe your spouse deserves it. Give it quickly and show your love and mercy towards your spouse (*Isaiah 56:4 and Micah 6:8*). I am certain that you can think of a time when you had to be forgiven and received not only forgiveness but mercy as well (*Matthew 5:7*). You cannot receive forgiveness if you are not willing to give it in return (*Matthew 6:15*). Just think about what Jesus did for us on the cross; it should make you more than willing to forgive your spouse.

Always remember that once you forgive your spouse; the forgiven situation is forgotten as the Lord does for us. It is not used as a weapon against your spouse in the future. "*I, even I, am He who blots out your transgressions for My own sake; and I will not remember your sins*" (*Isaiah 43:25*). When it is finally over, consider it dead to your relationship and move on to a brighter future together.

Growing Spiritually

Restoring and keeping your marriage has to begin with a foundation in the Word of God. You may not have been saved when you got married and you may not be saved now, but you need to head down that road now! God is the only way to restore your marriage and keep it whole. We should be seeking Jesus for spiritual maturity all of our lives. Think about where God has brought you from in your marriage and life. Does this thought make you desire to be closer to Him? Pray for each other continuously and teach each other the same (*1 Samuel 12:23-24*).

One of the most beautiful things that I share with my husband is our salvation. I know that I am not going to never have to leave him or vice-versa except for a short time when we die. Because of being saved through our acceptance of Jesus Christ and Faithfulness we will have everlasting life with Jesus after we leave this earth (*Matthew 19:29*). I will have my husband forever. Be steadfast in the Lord and claim your victory now in the flesh and spirit, and later with your soul. How beautiful is salvation?

Seeking God in your marriage is not really an option if you want success. We know that we have to seek Him first and His righteousness in order to have everything else added to it (*Matthew 6:33*). Our relationship on earth and in Heaven is dependent on it. Married Christians must serve the Lord; study the Bible; and pray for spiritual growth together.

Resolving Conflicts

All differences, arguments, disagreements and intolerances must be talked about and resolved. If there are old conflicts in your relationship, get those out of the way first. Start fresh, and make sure that you resolve all new conflicts immediately. The Bible tells us that when we resolve conflicts between each other that we gain favor, which is exactly what we want in our marriage (*Matthew 18:15*). Do not allow old situations or new situations to become an intrusion or disruption in your relationship. God has given us away to deal with it and instructed us to talk to each other to resolve problems. Just do it and be obedient.

Romance and Sex

To start, Christian Marriages need romance and sex to be fulfilled. The marriage bed is undefiled and you should enjoy each other as much as possible and never deprive each other of one another's body. Your Biblical romantic journey may begin with the *Song of Solomon chapter 1* where you will learn how to be romantic. Here we see kind words being spoken such as *"you are beautiful"* or *"your name is like perfumed oil."* Sweet words are always nice to hear. *Verse 14* states "My *beloved is to me a cluster of henna blossoms."* We can read the *Song of Solomon* to see examples of love, attraction, romance, conflict, courtship, and virtue. This is one of the reasons why I love God so much because he anticipated every need and provided for it.

A beautiful Word comes from *Proverbs 5:15-19* where we are told that there is no beauty like the sex of marriage. It also tells us not to share this intimacy with anyone outside of marriage. And man should allow his wife to be his fountain of blessing. I cannot impress upon you enough to always share yourselves with each other. Intimacy and sex strengthens your love, so be as strong as you can be! Have you submitted today?

Husbands and Wives Do so Much Wrong

Are you perfect? There is no one perfect but God, do not be hypocritical. The Bible tells us that we need to clean ourselves up before we begin to criticize anyone else (*Matthew 7:5*). I dare you to present yourself perfect while finding fault with your spouse. Understand that you both have faults, but you have an opportunity through Jesus to make yourselves so much better and enjoy each other all the days of your life. Go to God when things seem hard and praise Him when he brings you out. He asked us to *"Come to Me, all you who labor and are heavy laden, and I will give you rest. Take My yoke upon you and learn from Me, for I am gentle and lowly in heart, and you will find rest for your souls"* (Matthew 11:28-29). We have a means of restoring our relationships if we will only ask and receive that restoration.

In *2 Corinthians* we are warned not to be unequally yoked. Saved with unsaved cannot fellowship or share together. Married people are the exception to this rule because you are commanded to hold up your unbelieving spouse until such time that they come into the fold. Love them and show them mercy. I am sure you remember when you were not saved. You must love each other and not just with a warm touch or something similar. Love is a mirror of Jesus' love for us. It is not selfish, rude, jealous, contemptuous, full of pride, arrogant, dishonest, nasty, cruel, angry… Shall I go on? The love you must have is sacrificial in attitude and action. Love is never-ending and you should never have a mind to quit on each other.

Challenges

We are going to face quite a few challenges in our marriage, but they all can be overcome with a little effort on our part. I do say "little" because if you are serving the same God that I am; you already have the victory over everything of malice that you can imagine. Nothing can triumph over you or your marriage. Here you will find some of the common challenges and suggestions for dealing with them through Jesus Christ.

Extended Family

The siblings and in-laws of a marriage tend to pose a naturally and recurring problem if it is not handled properly. For the wife, she must understand that it is difficult for any Mother to give her son to another woman. There is always going to be something that you are not doing quite right or things that you may not do quite like she did. Continue to show her love and avoid confrontation with her. This is not a problem because your husband has forsaken his Mother and Father for you as God commanded. Have Faith in your husband that he will not place anyone in front of you including his Mother. You both need to discuss it; agree and the wife should allow her husband to handle the situation.

Outside Children

Maybe you or your spouse has one or more outside children. In our current society this has become a growing concern. This issue should be discussed prior to the marriage to ensure that ground rules are established and agreed upon upfront making the transition easier for you and the kids. This includes the rules for the outside Mother and Father. Remember the intrusion rule? Communication will play the largest role in keeping order in your home which is paramount. Neither the husband nor wife should allow children inside or outside to rule the house. Peace has to be made between the husband and wife regarding all children and the agreements must be adhered to unless you both agree to another arrangement. Do not forget to seek guidance from God initially.

Money Matters

How many times have I heard that all of the arguments were about money? My response to that is #1 are you spending your money wisely on things that money *has* to be spent on and #2 if you only have a certain amount of money and you are aware of it, then there is nothing to argue about. Ladies and gentleman taking care of a household is difficult and you are going to have to sacrifice some things you may desire in order to sufficiently do that. This may be your time with an extra job in the evenings or you may have to learn how to cut or perm your own hair. Go back and read the definition of love. Married people sacrifice out of love to ensure the well-being of the family. This cannot be done without working together and communication. Money is never a feasible reason for a disagreement. NEVER!

I understand that you may have been accustomed to a certain way of living at one point in your marriage and things may have changed. You have to change as well. God will provide for you; just remember that while you are going through your change. Is it so bad to use a bargain brand every now and then to save your money and ultimately your marriage? It is all about how you are thinking about it. Mindset and attitude are paramount. Most of us tend to live above our actual means anyway; therefore it is likely that we are going to experience money issues. Talk to each other and simply work it out; give a little and get a lot.

The next example of money issues is not something that I heard in a counseling session; but this is one of my personal experiences. My son will soon be 18 years old and I am not sure if he even knows that his Father and I used to sell plasma to buy formula-milk for him. At that time we were both active duty military and simply did not have enough money to keep that child in milk. Boy could he eat! We laugh about it now and it was hard, but we did it together. We did not have what we wanted but we had what we needed and never lost a single pound. Consequently I say, never quit on each other, especially about something as silly as money. And do not play the blame game because you are in the situation together. Remember, you cannot buy love, peace, or happiness. The most important thing to us then and now is being together. I look at my son now and he was worth every drop we sold! This is also another testament that trouble comes but it will pass.

Unreasonable Expectations

We spoke about unreasonable expectations earlier. Why would you expect your husband to do a deed or task that you *KNOW* he cannot accomplish and then beat him up over it? Silly woman, learn your husband, learn your husband, learn your husband. Then after you learn what he can and cannot do, encourage him and let him know that it is ok because you love him. Remember these are the same things he could not do when you first got married. Time has not changed his abilities. He may be on a road to improvement in some area and that is great, but your job is not to point out his faults, but to encourage and support him every day of his life.

My husband is a sweet soul but he has an issue with going to school, which is one of my passions. He told me when we first met that he barely made it out of high school and he was not thinking about going any further. This was disheartening to me because I love school and wanted to continue. Twenty years later I have completed four degrees and now working on my second doctoral degree, praise the Lord! But my husband is happy and content with his high school diploma and so am I. I love him for what is *TO* me not what he can *GIVE* me or what society thinks about him and his education level. He excels at his craft and I am so proud of him. The amount of love, attention, and concern that I have gotten from that man, even when I did not deserve it, is worth more to me than anything I can name. Wives, be thankful for the husband that you have and stop imagining what you don't have. The blessings that are meant for you are the only ones that you need and should enjoy. Believe it and be happy.

People Viruses

Your friends and associates will be like viruses to your marriage if you allow it. Handle your own affairs in your own house between you and your husband. Of course, you may have that one friend that you know has your best interest at heart and she/he is a practicing Christian and not the devil testing you. Do not be fooled by those friends that you have had for many years because these are the very ones that will infect your relationship quicker than a new acquaintance. Be careful of advice and seek God before you tear into your spouse for any reason. Remember just as you do not want him putting anyone before you; do not put your friends before him. God will put things into perspective for you. Never argue with one another, but find a way to talk about issues involving outside people. Evil will thrive in the midst of the trouble you *ALLOW* in your house. Hang a "keep out" sign and enforce it.

Of course you can have friends! The friend of one spouse is also the friend of the other spouse OR the friendship cannot and should not exist. How can it be feasible for the "best friend" of the wife to dislike the husband? What a deal breaker. Remember how the husband took care of the Mother-in-law? The wife has to take care of the excommunication of this friend. An agreement must happen between you and your husband that you are not going to let anyone or anything, especially this friend, fracture your relationship.

We all need that person that we can talk to about "stuff" and that is fine. I have a girlfriend just like that and I do not speak with her often, but when I do it is "off-the-chain!" I can yell with her; cry with her and it is ok. When I am done she always asks me do I feel better. I tell her "yep," now I am going to pray. She is unassuming, understands and allows me to have a sounding board. Sometimes you need to tell someone how you feel about something or someone before you actually say it "live." You just may be wrong, imagine that? She might be the person to help put things into prospective and realize how silly it was from the start. Women generally need this outlet more than men, but it is beneficial either way. If you have genuine friends that love you with a genuine love; keep them in your lives. These folks are not like viruses and will not seek to infect and destroy your marriage.

Remember you have made relationships with people in the past and will continue to do so in the future, but the most important relationships consist of your husband and God.

Reminders

Pray

Do not ever stop praying. Pray singularly and pray together. You may both be saved or one of you may not be saved *YET*. Hold up your unbelieving spouse and pray harder for him/her and your marriage continuously. Pray for your own strength to continue. Wives, God even spoke to us separately on this subject. He said that we should continue to be good wives and obey the Word and our husbands will be *"won by the conversation of the wives"* (1 Peter 3:1). Use your God given power in your relationship through pray and continued obedience. Do not try and force the issue because he will come when he is ready.

Pride yourself in being intimate in your prayers. Pray about everything no matter how small it may be and do it together. I generally tell my husband and anybody that is speaking with me; either I prayed about what we are talking about or I am going to pray about what we are talking about. Either way some praying is going to get done. Make it a part of your day every day.

Never quit

Marriage is a permanent commitment and there is no room to change your mind a few times before you get it right. Enter into it fully aware that you are making a commitment to God through your marriage vows. The commitment belongs to Him and so do you. Lean on the Lord for your strength as he will never leave you or forsake you. He promises to direct you in all that you do; especially in your marriage (*Proverbs 3:5-6*). Just trust Him. Whatever comes out of your mouth; you will keep as not only a promise to the one you said it to but to God Himself (*Deuteronomy 23:23*). You should walk around and say "23 23" over and over again to help you remember. You must keep your commitment and take it as serious as you take anything else Holy and sanctified.

Tame your mouth

Mind how you speak to your husband. Oh yes, it matters. The Bible tells us to be quick to listen and slow to speak and to anger (*James 1:19*). Take heed to what you are going to say and how you are going to say it; before you actually say it. If you are unsure; keep your mouth closed until you can speak with love and kindness. Every time you have a desire to "go off" on your husband does not give you a license to do so. It is better to speak when it is time to speak and not before. When words are spoken correctly at the right time; they are "good," even if the information given is bad (*Proverbs 15:23*).

Many times I sit and listen at couples argue about one thing or the other and the words they use are purely ugly. Did you know that every time you utter a word you let the listener into your heart? Think about some of the things you have said to your husband; were these words from your heart? If so, do you need to ask for cleansing of your heart? Your speech has to be worthy of Jesus Christ (*Philippians 1:27*). How can you say such ugly words to a person that you love and have committed your entire existence to in front of God? In *Proverbs 12:18* we see that your words are like a sword to people. Is it your intent to cut your husband when you speak to him? We have to speak life into our spouse although we may be angry. Do what the Lord says to do, not what you want to do. The results will be better, guaranteed.

Start a union

Your home can not stand if it is divided against itself. Just as you and your husband cannot have a successful relationship until you realize that you are one flesh. So start a union against any attackers. First, let everyone you know in on the movement. Let them know that your house will be united at all costs and no one can weaken the structure. Make it a goal that you work towards every day. Pray for strength for your union and ask God to continue to bless it. People may not agree with it or understand it, but you are responsible for keeping it together not them.

Strength and Endurance

Did you know that all of your newly found tasks, attitude, mindset, works, and prayers will not work without Jesus Christ in your life? Jesus is the vine and we are the branches and with Him we will do good things, but without Him we can do nothing (*John 15:5*). When you are feeling weak; don't quit but lean on Jesus even more and He will not fail you. Do not try and understand problems that are higher than you.

Jesus thinks on a Heavenly level which is impossible for us to understand. Give it to the Lord with all your heart (*Proverbs 3:5*).

There are going to be times when you will have to suffer. Love is longsuffering. Look at Jesus Christ's life. When you have to make a decision between something out in the world and your spouse; the spouse will win every time. You will certainly depart from an evil thing to go with Christ (*Philippians 1:23*). When you fight the good fight all of your treasures are already laid up in Heaven for you. Your suffering will include loss, death, evildoers, punishment, depression, harm, disobedient children and many more things, but we are told to continue to love and not be mad about it (*Ephesians 4:2*). Take up *YOUR* cross daily following Jesus and denying yourself (*Luke 9:23*). Believe that your suffering is a passing event just as other things have passed in your life. Stay strong.

Trust that the Lord is your strength (*Psalm 28:8*). Know that the strength that you exude in keeping your family is honorable and beautiful to God (*Psalm 96:6*). Pray for ongoing majesty and beauty before God as this will be pleasing to Him. Continue to exercise patience while waiting for the Lord and let Him see that you have Faith. The things that we continue to hope for and cannot see are a product of our Faith (*Romans 8:25*). God knows that we are not sure exactly what to pray for and he knows what we need and what we want before we do; therefore have no worries if you have not prayed the correct prayer. It will still happen for you.

Children

I do not have the opportunity to focus much on children for spending massive amounts of time with the Momma and Daddy, but children are an important part of our married life and deserve some attention. The Lord has made sure that children are considered over and over in the Bible regarding how they should behave and how we should raise them. One of the most beautiful scriptures about children is found in *Matthew 18:14* where Jesus said that it was not the will of the Father that even one perish. Although we know that the context was about sheep; He would leave 99 safe to go rescue one that was lost. That is the way he feels about us and is how we should feel about our children.

A home is not a reflection of how big it is or how much it costs. A home is all about what is going on inside. Has the wife built a home in which to teach her children the ways of the Lord; a place for nurture and care; and an environment where love flourishes (*Proverbs 14:1*)? Some women will not agree, but this is part of our job and we will be held accountable for the home. Children are to know the scriptures early in their lives, learning how to be wise and able to make decisions about salvation (*2 Timothy 3:15*) AND we must train our children the way that we know they must be trained to protect them when they are adults (*Proverbs 22:6*) AND we are to tell our children of the Lord so that they continue to tell it to their families for generations (*Joel 1:3*). These things are not options for parents. A good wife is also a good Mother!

The Do(s) of a Good Marriage

The husbands and wives that I have counseled have been grateful for the messages they received and have been so wonderful with their support. Unfortunately the messages and other resources are long and involved. I require that they do lots of reading and studying of the scriptures that I give them. Although, they are not tested, so to speak, I do insist that we have discussions after they have meditated on the Word. Recently, they have been hinting around at study materials that are shorter and can be completed in less time. I will say this and move on; Jesus is very long and involved and you cannot begin to scratch the surface of his depth over a few hours a month. You are going to have to get cozy with the Word of God and stay with it until Jesus comes back. That means for Life!

However, since I try to practice servant leadership, I will do whatever I have to do to ensure that the Word is getting across to all those that want to hear it. I have been asked to do "shortcuts" to my messages on relationships and marriages and I agreed. I have compiled a couple of "to-do" lists; one for the husband and one for the wife.

Husband – Do these things without fail

#1 (*Genesis 2:24*). Your highest honor will go to God and next to your wife. There is no other on earth that can compare to the Faithfulness, duty, loyalty and commitment you will show to your wife.

#2 (*1 Peter 3:7*). You will give your wife the highest respect and honor as your equal heir of the grace of life.

#3 (*Song of Solomon 5:10-16*). You will maintain and hold your wife's love by same means that you obtained it. If you sang songs continue to sing; if you bought roses send a flower; if you whispered in her ear continue to do that and any other thing.

#4 (*Proverbs 31:10-11 and Philippians 2:3*). You will tell your wife every chance you get how much you appreciate her as your wife and how much she means to you.

#5 (*Proverbs 5:15-20*). You will keep your eyes, hands, and mind on your wife and not across the way! Make sure that your wife's breasts are the only ones that you allow to satisfy you.

#6 (*Ephesians 6:4*). You will make sure that you include your wife in your preparation for rearing and disciplining the children. Share the responsibility and submit to one another and come to an agreement concerning all things.

#7 (*Matthew 5:37*). Whatever you tell your wife you are going to do; just do it. Tell her *yes* or *no* and mean it. You will preserve the integrity and honesty in your relationship.

#8 (*Genesis 21:12*). LISTEN to your wife.

#9 (*Song of Solomon 8:1 and Esther 5:3*). You will not hold anything from your wife. You will kiss and hug her when you are near her and give her your treasures; be it money, a nibble off your plate or anything else.

The husband "*to do*" list only contains nine items; therefore you should be able to reference them quickly and comply even quicker! I am certain that your wives will be happy with their great Godly husbands. I cannot guarantee submission nights will increase, but I will continue to pray!

Wife - Do these things without fail

#1 (*Philippians 4:11*). You will stop expecting your husband to give you more than he has to give. Be content, grateful, supportive and encouraging always.

#2 (*Proverbs 14:1*). You will be proud of the husband you have and respect him in all that you do by building a home for your family to thrive within.

#3 (*Philippians 2:3*). You will make sure that your husband knows how much you love and respect him as your husband.

#4 (*Proverbs 27:15*). You will not badger, pester, irritate, hassle or otherwise harass your husband. Do not be a drip!

#5 (*1 Peter 5:9*). You will keep all of your nosy friends out of your marriage and out of your husband's face at all times.

#6 (*1 Peter 3:4*). You will not **yell** your dissatisfaction to your husband but will talk to your husband to receive comfort and agreement.

#7 (*1 Corinthians 7:3-5*). You will show him love every chance that you get. Kiss and hug him as warmly as possible.

#8 (*Ezekiel 16:32*). You will check with your husband above all in all things allowing no man to have a chance with you.

#9 (*1 Peter 3:5*). You will continue to keep yourself beautiful and sexy for your husband only.

#10 (*1 Peter 3:6*). You will submit as the body to the head with all of your heart following your husband wherever he may go.

The wife "*to-do*" list is complete with ten items that you must accomplish to ensure abounding success in your marriage. By the way, I believe that your husband would appreciate it if you would double the current submission rate. Amen!

Dr Chele's Final Commentary

I am so prayerful for all of you that decided to turn to God for answers and restoration of your relationships. I believe God values His creation of marriage and I am blessed and honored to be able to help people preserve it through His Word. It is my deepest hope that you will use this book to further study the Word of God and if you have not began your journey; use it to begin your studying. I believe with all my heart that Jesus is the light and for those that seek and find Him darkness will be no more. Step into the light!

To all of the single women everywhere, I know that it is hard for you in your state of "wait," but it is worth the wait. God has never been late. Please make up your mind to wait on Him.

For the married women, please slow down and smell *YOUR* roses no matter how few or many. They are yours to be proud of and cherish. I am praying for married women and men every where to find peace, contentment, happiness, love and restoration through their service to the Lord. **Repent. Accept Jesus. Be saved! Amen.**

www.ingramcontent.com/pod-product-compliance
Lightning Source LLC
Chambersburg PA
CBHW080252170426
43192CB00014BA/2649